Children
302.231
Dell

Dell, Pamela

Understanding social
media

$27.99

DATE DUE

DEC - - 2018

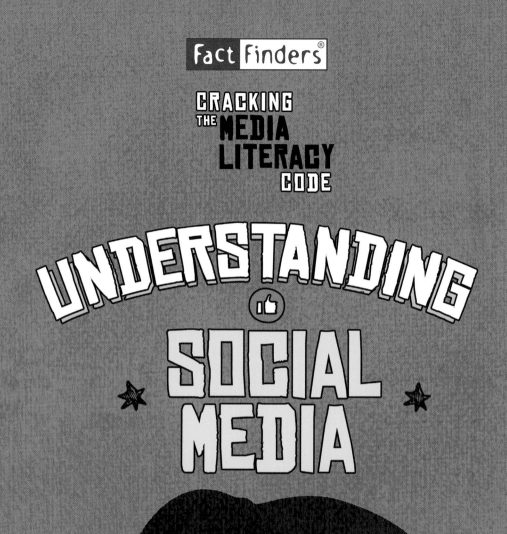

Fact Finders®

CRACKING THE MEDIA LITERACY CODE

UNDERSTANDING 👍 SOCIAL MEDIA

BY PAMELA DELL

CONSULTANT:
ROBERT L. MCCONNELL, PHD

CAPSTONE PRESS
a capstone imprint

Fact Finders Books are published by Capstone Press
1710 Roe Crest Drive, North Mankato, Minnesota 56003
www.mycapstone.com

Library of Congress Cataloging-in-Publication Data
ISBN 978-1-5435-2706-3 (hardcover)
ISBN 978-1-5435-2714-8 (paperback)
ISBN 978-1-5435-2722-3 (ebook PDF)

Editorial Credits
Michelle Bisson, editor; Russell Griesmer, designer; Jennifer Bergstrom, production artist; Morgan Walters,
media researcher; Tori Abraham, production specialist

Photo Credits
Alamy: PPJF Military Collection, 27; ASSOCIATED PRESS: Axel Heimken, 11; Getty Images: Kevin Mazur,
6, Mark Boster, 16; iStockphoto: damedeeso, 7, gmutlu, 14; Shutterstock: Alisara Zilch, cover, design element
throughout, balabolka, cover, design element throughout, catwalker, 15, chanpipat, 25, charles taylor, 21,
Eladora, (head) cover, karen roach, 29, MacrovectorBottom of Form, nopporn, 20, notkoo, 5, o Samsara o,
24, panuwat phimpha, 18, Rawpixel.com, 26, SpeedKingz, 28, topform, cover, design element throughout;
Wikimedia: Jscott, 8, Laurens van Lieshout, 13

Printed in the United States of America.
PA021

TABLE OF CONTENTS

CHAPTER 1

WHAT IS MEDIA LITERACY?

Think about it. You have the whole world in one device. Or quite a lot of it, anyway. Everyone who has a smartphone, tablet, or computer can connect to the Internet. They can share photos and post opinions. They can send a string of texts or emails. They can stay in close touch with their whole social circle.

The wider world is easy to get to as well. All it takes is a few keystrokes, voice commands, or clicks. People can find global news, entertainment, and just about any information they need. We're all citizens of the digital world. That means media literacy is more important than ever. But what does media literacy mean?

DID YOU KNOW?

Types of media have three main purposes—to persuade, to entertain, and to inform. An important part of media literacy is having the smarts to tell which is which. Media literacy is the ability to gather information from all media sources and analyze it intelligently.

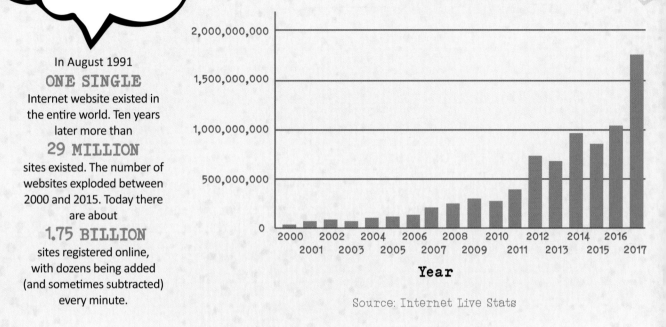

WEBSITE EXPLOSION!

In August 1991 **ONE SINGLE** Internet website existed in the entire world. Ten years later more than **29 MILLION** sites existed. The number of websites exploded between 2000 and 2015. Today there are about **1.75 BILLION** sites registered online, with dozens being added (and sometimes subtracted) every minute.

Total Number of Websites

Year

Source: Internet Live Stats

We get information from various forms of media, including newspapers, magazines, radio, and TV. We also view billboards, flyers, and posters. And don't forget the Internet, with its 1.75 billion or so websites worldwide. And that doesn't include the millions of separate social media accounts on sites such as Snapchat, Instagram, Facebook, and Twitter. That's a lot of media.

⭐ analyze—to make a detailed examination and explanation of something

⭐ social media—websites and software applications that allow users to connect through the Internet

Being bombarded by media has become a part of modern life. So how does a person make sense of the information overload and sort through it wisely? How do you find the information you need while avoiding what is useless, distracting, and downright untrue? How do you keep from being fooled by ads that look like news stories?

The answer is media literacy. It is a skill that helps people weed out false information and tall tales. And keeps them from being caught in a faker's web.

DID YOU KNOW?

In 2016 an 11-year-old boy did something that was both amazing and successful. Sidney Keys III started Books n Bros (booksnbros.com). It is a reading club to encourage literacy among African American boys. Thanks to social media, Sidney's efforts went viral. And he won CNN's Young Wonder award.

Sidney Keys III

Media literacy also allows you to focus on what is useful. For example, think of all the pets that are separated from their families during natural disasters or other troubles. In the predigital age not much could be done to help. But

People have found their lost pets after posting about them on social media.

now Internet users turn to social media to reunite lost animals with their people. It has resulted in many heartwarming success stories. Who wouldn't want to be part of—or even start—such a positive project now that it's possible? Understanding how to use media can help.

predigital—before the time of computer technology

reunite—to bring together again

CHAPTER 2

THE ROOTS OF INTERNET CONNECTION

In January 1978 Chicago was hit with one of the city's worst snowstorms. Nobody could get around. But the Great Blizzard of 1978 gave two young computer programmers a chance to go down in history. While the storm raged, Ward Christensen and Randy Suess began work on something that would change the world.

Ward Christensen with the first BBS

It was a software program called CBBS, the computer bulletin board system. It was later shortened to BBS. It was a groundbreaking moment. Back then the Internet was very small and few people had computers. But some people who did could now connect to Christensen's BBS. To do so they used their landline telephones and a dial-up modem. Users posted news and announcements, much as they might on a bulletin board hanging on a wall. They could send each other messages.

The whole system was very slow. But its value came in connecting a large group of people in more than one geographical area. Pretty soon BBS networks were cropping up in one city after another.

By the early 1990s more and more people had logged onto the networks. They were excited by the possibilities of being connected through cyberspace. The roots of social media had sprouted.

 modem—a piece of electronic equipment that sends information between computers by telephone lines

cyberspace—the online world of computer networks

The first message board lit a great spark. But the slow and clunky BBS model was doomed. By the mid-1990s people were discovering new and better ways to connect with one another on their computers. One of the first ways was email, which quickly gained popularity. Email was great for both personal and business uses.

America Online (AOL) was one of the first and most successful companies to offer email service to people for a fee. AOL took online communication another giant leap forward in 1997. It offered users AIM—America Online Instant Messaging. Now people could chat with friends in real time, right on their computer screens. While they talked, they could do other things as well. They could even trade IMs with more than one person at a time.

DID YOU KNOW?

One of the very first instant messaging systems for kids was created in 1983. Its creator was Mark Jenks, a Milwaukee, Wisconsin, high school student. It was called "Talk." Once students at his high school logged in, they could send each other private messages.

This AOL icon became well known around the world.

Other companies soon tried to follow AOL's lead. But in the late 1990s and early 2000s AOL dominated. Sometimes as many as 18 million users were sending and receiving instant messages at the same time. But then communication methods changed and AOL lost its grip on the big numbers.

Instant messaging wasn't the only tool being developed. Companies began to create social media and gaming sites of all kinds. Everyone wanted to outdo AOL and AIM. The competitors added fun features and their own messaging systems. The sites began to draw many users.

A new Internet sensation launched in May 1997, at exactly the same time AIM appeared. Called Six Degrees, it offered instant messaging. It also gave users the power to create personal profiles and friends lists. They could even search each other's friends lists. Today that's no big deal. But in the 1990s, it was unheard of. Word spread quickly and users flocked to Six Degrees. At its peak the site had more than 1 million registered members.

Six Degrees lasted only a few years. Still, its early success pushed other companies to build their own social networking sites. As one rose, others fell. The social media wars were on.

Six Degrees of Separation

Six Degrees got its name from the idea that only six degrees of separation exist between any two people on Earth. In other words, you and five of your acquaintances connect to everyone—including any celebrity. Research proves the point—almost! In 2006 Microsoft studied the records of 30 billion electronic conversations among 180 million people in various countries. It was about half the world's instant messaging traffic at the time. They found that it took about 6.6 hops to connect any two pairs of people messaging online.

There's even a game based on the idea, called Six Degrees of Kevin Bacon. Players try to find links between Hollywood star Kevin Bacon and any other actor, dead or alive. The idea is that it shouldn't take more than six steps of connection.

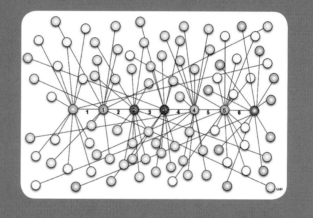

CHAPTER 3

THE SOCIAL MEDIA EXPLOSION

A social networking site called Friendster took the lead in the social media wars in 2002. But its popularity didn't last. Only a year later, the young social media crowd turned to MySpace. Two former Friendster members created it.

MySpace had many great familiar features and new ones as well. Users could create a custom-designed profile page of their own. Then they could add music, videos, and a page featuring pictures of their "top friends." All this attracted millions of registered members worldwide.

Friendster was a pioneer in social media.

But the real monster among social media options would soon take over the field. That monster, called The Facebook, launched in 2004. It was a network to connect Harvard University students to each other. It then quickly spread to other universities around the country. What became better known as Facebook was opened to everyone in 2006. And the rest is social media history.

Mark Zuckerberg

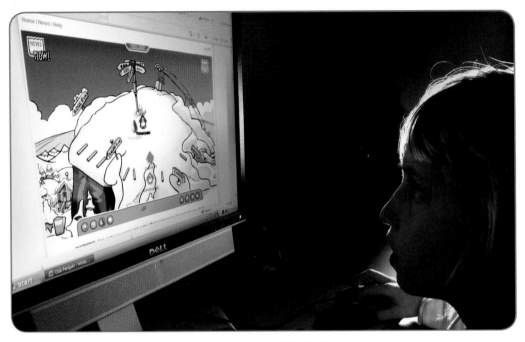

Club Penguin was a popular site with kids.

Demand for Facebook grew quickly. In April 2008, two years after it became open to the public, Facebook beat out MySpace in the number of unique visits worldwide. Facebook reported that by the end of 2017 it had 2.2 billion active monthly users worldwide. That means billions of people were logging in at least once a month.

Facebook set its age limit for registering at 13. But kids had other choices for connecting online. One of the most successful was Club Penguin, a virtual world launched in 2005.

Almost nothing like it had been tried before. Club Penguin ruled with its target audience for nearly 12 years. Users created and named their own penguin avatars. Then a whole fun world opened up. The popular game ended in 2017, replaced by Club Penguin Island. But gaming had become another big way to connect and socialize on the Internet.

 Cutting Edge Social Media

Before the term *social media* even came into use, a multimedia company called Purple Moon made computer games with a social aspect for preteen girls. Users shared thousands of private messages through an internal "postcard" system. They also traded digital icons called virtual treasures. Purple Moon, launched in 1997, proved how popular social media could be. For the two years it operated, the site had about 240,000 registered users. Mattel dominated the preteen gaming industry for girls with its Barbie games. It bought Purple Moon and then shut it down.

 virtual—not physically existing but made by computer software to seem real

 target audience—a particular group that a book, movie, TV show, or product aims at

 avatar—a computer icon made to stand for a person

Do you want a fantasy world where you role-play with thousands of others around the world? And do you want to chat with them at the same time? That's what online role-playing games offer computer users. These games are another popular way people connect and socialize on the Internet.

Sites that allow users in various locations to play games together have a long history. The first multiuser dungeon game came along in 1978 in the United States. By 1979 it had an international base of players. In 1987 a multiplayer adventure game called Habitat launched. Then, in the late 1990s came massive multiplayer role-playing games (MMORPGs). MMORPGs had realistic, three-dimensional color graphics and great sound effects that users couldn't resist. Many of the virtual worlds became massive hits in the real world.

Online games let users live in a fanasy world
where they can be heroes.

Everquest was one of the first and biggest. Released
by Sony Online Entertainment in 1999, it led the pack
until 2004. Then other MMORPGs overtook Everquest.
Every game developer was looking for ways to outdo
and out-flash the others. By the turn of the 21st century,
gaming was a very profitable business. And it still is.

CHAPTER 4

SHARING—A MIXED BAG

Gaming is only one of the many ways to connect online. Social media is another, often with big benefits. It's one of the best and fastest ways to raise money for important causes and favorite projects. Social media also helps people easily keep up to date on who's doing what. People use social media to find old friends or make new ones. People also use social media to keep up with one another, and with the news.

Social media connects people around the globe who would otherwise never meet.

But sometimes sharing can lead a person down a wrong road. Here's one way that can happen: You come across a piece of information you agree with, disagree with, or just feel strongly about. What do you do? You share it. And so does everybody else.

Understanding the difference between true and fake news is the first step in media literacy.

But often the stuff being shared is not true. It is fake but posing as real, fact-based information. Most people don't stop to research the facts on such posts. They just pass them on. This is how false information spreads so far and wide and ends up being thought of as the truth. Everyone believes it, even if it's completely made up. And that's bad.

Here's the bottom line: Always think twice about what and with whom you share information. Sites such as Facebook may be the place to go for news about family and friends. But they're also loaded with false information in many forms. Facebook has been host to thousands of fake political ads and news stories.

DID YOU KNOW?

From 2015 to 2017 a Russian organization called Internet Research Agency placed at least 3,000 fake ads on Facebook, most of them political. About 10 million people saw the ads. The most popular fake U.S. political stories on Facebook in 2016 got 10.6 million shares and comments.

FAKE NEWS IS A REAL PROBLEM

Total Facebook engagement for top 20 election stories (August-Election Day)

Fake news   8.7 million

Mainstream news   7.3 million

Source: Buzzsumo via Buzzfeed

Much of the junk news comes from Russia and other countries trying to sway the opinions of Americans. Facebook's founder, Mark Zuckerberg, is working with the U.S. government to stop the meddling. They're looking for ways to reduce the problem and protect users.

But meanwhile, before you share anything, examine it closely and critically. Make sure it's accurate information. Do your own resaearch or look for information or other sites that have a fact-checking service. Don't just believe everything you read.

Learn to tell the difference between fake news and real news. And remember that opinion and fact are two different things. A news story isn't fake just because you don't like what it says. Many politicians label facts they disagree with as fake news. The information may not be fake. It might just be that they don't like it.

Clickbait Crazy

The term *clickbait* is getting a lot of play lately—because the Internet is loaded with it. Clickbait is a link that makes you so curious you can't help clicking through to the linked content. Maybe the bait was an outrageous headline or a fantastic bargain. The clickbait might lead you to a site that tries to sell you something. Or to a site that makes money on every view. Word to the wise: Don't take the bait!

⭐ accurate—agreeing exactly with truth or a standard

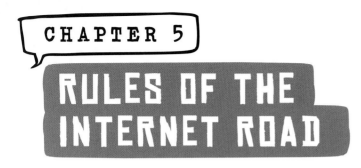

CHAPTER 5

RULES OF THE INTERNET ROAD

Social media has given young people a much wider and more global viewpoint. Sharing and declaring one's news to an ever-increasing list of friends is hard to resist. But if you're not careful it's easy to get caught in an online trap.

In other words, some social media conduct today could have not-so-great effects down the road. Be sure to follow a few worthwhile rules to prevent making a wrong move when you're interacting with others online.

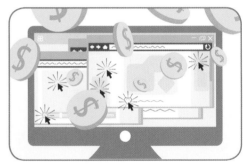

People can use your private information to make money, so be careful what you post.

DID YOU KNOW?

A lot of kids think it's safe to share things **anonymously** on apps like Snapchat. The idea is that the messages only appear for a short time so you're safe. Think again. Cyberthieves and bullies can easily take screenshots and photos of posts and photos in the short time they're available to view.

Everybody wants to feel connected to their closest friends. Social media makes that a breeze. But when you post every detail about yourself and your life, unwanted eyes may also be watching. It is very important to check your online privacy settings. Ask an adult to help. Many social media sites make all their users' information public by default. Anyone with an Internet connection can see it. That means you have to change this yourself if you don't want everyone to see all your information. Many sites make it easy. They help you keep unwanted Internet users from seeing your pictures, posts, or personal information. So do it!

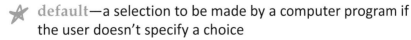

Why Set Limits?

Many popular social media sites have an age limit of 13 at which users can join. But sometimes it's as high as 17 or older. Companies set age limits to keep kids away from thieves or **predators** who want to harm them. Even if you create a secret, fake account, people you don't know may still get and use your real data. Many times it's just advertisers who want to sell you things. But not always.

 anonymously—without naming or identifying

default—a selection to be made by a computer program if the user doesn't specify a choice

predator—a person who goes after someone or something in order to take advantage in a negative way

It is usually up to the user to set up levels of privacy.

On Snapchat, for example, users have multiple security choices when it comes to who can view your story or send you Snaps. On Instagram, the default is that anyone can view whatever you post. So you must choose the "Private Account" setting. Otherwise, your pictures could end up in anyone's Internet search.

It might not seem like a big deal in many cases. But let's say you post a picture of yourself laughing at a crying baby. And then you try to get a babysitting job. Chances are someone who might hire you has seen the pictures. Or maybe you're applying for a spot in a selective school or in a special program. It's a good bet the decision-makers will look for you on social media.

There's a big difference between a real friend reaching out and a complete stranger wanting to find out more about you. So beyond privacy settings, common-sense rules

The military ran an ad campaign called "Think Before You Post" to help protect its social media users.

apply. When interacting online, never send pictures or reveal your address, phone number, or other personal information to someone you don't know well or at all. Even when you do know them, send the information privately rather than on a social media site.

DID YOU KNOW?

Direct messaging is popular with cyberthieves who place links that can lead to harmful downloads. Never click on a message from someone you don't know.

 surveillance—the act of keeping very close watch on someone

Do you know what cyberbullying is? Have you ever done it? Lots of kids have. Cyberbullying is bullying. But it is carried out over digital devices—computers, tablets, and cell phones. It happens on social media sites, in chat rooms, through texts and emails, and on apps. It consists of mean and hurtful words or pictures. Its purpose is to shame, embarrass, or show a person in a negative way.

Cyberbullying may seem harmless but it often leads to depression.

Cyberbullying has become a huge problem. Because the Internet is always on, there's little relief for the targeted kids. If you are being bullied, go offline and talk to a trusted adult about what's being said about you.

DID YOU KNOW?

It's estimated that 28 percent of middle school and high school students have been victims of cyberbullying. Fewer than one in five incidents are reported.

Even if you've never experienced cyberbullying yourself, imagine what it must be like. No one deserves to suffer from bullying behavior.

You can help prevent cyberbullying! Don't do it and don't let your friends bully other kids.

Social media is a wonderful tool when used well. You can learn more about friends, and the world, and see cool pictures of pets. It's not so wonderful when it's used to spread false information or to hurt someone else. So—enjoy social media! Put your media literacy to work as an informed digital citizen.

Try This!

You have the choice to make a valuable difference in the world. Many young people have gotten public attention for tweeting positive comments instead. They use online video channels and other social media to do good things. They showcase talented friends, raise money for disease research, or organize food banks for the poor. There's no end to the good a person can do online.

GLOSSARY

accurate (ak-YUH-rit)—agreeing exactly with truth or a standard

analyze (AN-uh-lize)—to make a detailed examination and explanation of something

anonymously (uh-NON-i-mush-lee)—without naming or identifying

avatar (AV-uh-tahr)—a computer icon made to stand for a person

cyberspace (SY-buhr SPAYSS)—the online world of computer networks

default (duh-FAWLT)—a selection to be made by a computer program if the user doesn't specify a choice

modem (MOH-duhm)—a piece of electronic equipment that sends information between computers by telephone lines

predator (PRED-uh-tur)—a person who goes after someone or something in order to take advantage in a negative way

predigital (pree-DI-juh-tuhl)—before the time of computer technology

reunite (re-yu-NITE)—to bring together again

social media (SOH-shul MEE-dee-uh)—websites and software applications that allow users to connect through the Internet

surveillance (suhr-VAY-luhnss)—the act of keeping very close watch on someone

target audience (TAHR-git AW-dee-uhns)—a particular group that a book, movie, TV show, or product aims at

virtual (VIHR-choo-uhl)—not physically existing but made by computer software to seem real

READ MORE

Anton, Carrie. *A Smart Girl's Guide: Digital World: How to Connect, Share, Play, and keep Yourself Safe.* Middleton, Wisc.: American Girl Publishing, 2017.

McKenzie, Precious. *Library Skills and Internet Research.* Hitting the Books: Skills for Reading, Writing, and Research. Vero Beach, Fla.: Rourke Educational Media, 2014.

Minton, Eric. *Cyberbullies.* Stay Safe Online. New York: Powerkids Press, 2014.

CRITICAL THINKING QUESTIONS

1. What were two of the earliest developments in computer technology? What might have been the advantages of each?
2. How has digital technology changed the world for the better? What are some ways that have made it worse? Do you think it's a benefit to be able to be "wired" all the time? Why or why not?
3. What might cause a person to participate in cyberbullying? How can it can be reduced or prevented?

INTERNET SITES

Use FactHound to find Internet sites related to this book.

1. Visit *www.facthound.com*
2. Just type in 9781543527063 and go.

Super-cool stuff! Check out projects, games and lots more at
www.capstonekids.com

INDEX